Soft Drink
Hard Labour

Guatemalan Workers Take On Coca-Cola

Practical
ACTION
PUBLISHING

Latin America Bureau

This booklet has been endorsed by the following unions:

ACTT Association of Cinematograph, Television, and Allied Technicians
BFAWU Bakers, Food and Allied Workers Union*
FTAT Furniture, Timber and Allied Trades Union
GMBATU General, Municipal, Boilermakers and Allied Trades Union*
ISTC Iron and Steel Trades Confederation
IUF International Union of Food and Allied Workers' Associations
NALGO National and Local Government Officers Association
NCU National Communications Union
NGA National Graphical Association
NUJ National Union of Journalists
NUM National Union of Mineworkers
NUPE National Union of Public Employees
NUR National Union of Railwaymen*
SCPS Society of Civil and Public Servants
SOGAT Society of Graphical and Allied Trades
TGWU Transport and General Workers Union*
TASS Tobacco Sector. Technical, Administrative and Supervisory Section*
UCATT Union of Construction, Allied Trades and Technicians
URTU United Road Transport Union*
USDAW Union of Shop, Distributive and Allied Workers*

* IUF affiliates

Practical Action Publishing Ltd
25 Albert Street, Rugby, CV21 2SD, Warwickshire, UK
www.practicalactionpublishing.com

First published in 1987 by the Latin America Bureau (Research and Action) Ltd,
1 Arnwell Street, London EC1R 1UL

Digitized in 2015

The Latin America Bureau is an independent research and publishing
organisation. It works to broaden public understanding of issues of human
rights and social and economic justice in Latin America and the Caribbean.

Reprinted by Practical Action Publishing
Rugby, Warwickshire UK

ISBN 0 906156 33 5
ISBN 13: 9780906156339
ISBN Library Ebook: 9781909013803
Book DOI: http://dx.doi.org/10.3362/9781909013803

This booklet is published with the support of WOW Campaigns Ltd., the campaigning
associate of War on Want

Written by Mike Gatehouse and Miguel Angel Reyes
Editing and additional material by James Painter
Cover photograph by Jenny Matthews, design by Jan Brown

A catalogue record for this book is available from the British Library.

Since 1974, Practical Action Publishing has published and disseminated books and
information in support of international development work throughout the world.
Practical Action Publishing is a trading name of Practical Action Publishing Ltd
(Company Reg. No. 1159018), the wholly owned publishing company of Practical
Action. Practical Action Publishing trades only in support of its parent charity
objectives and any profits are covenanted back to Practical Action (Charity Reg.
No. 247257, Group VAT Registration No. 880 9924 76).

Guatemala

News about Guatemala rarely appears in British newspapers. Yet the country has been torn apart in recent years by a brutal civil war, in which the Guatemalan army has earned itself the reputation of being one of the worst human rights violators in the world. A British Parliamentary delegation which visited the country in 1984 concluded: 'In a thirty-year war against their own people, the Guatemalan military have created a nation of widows and orphans. Over 100,000 people have been killed and 38,000 disappeared.'

At the root of the conflict lie spectacular wealth and grinding poverty. A few very rich families and generals control the country's wealth, while the majority of Guatemala's eight million inhabitants - many of them indigenous Mayan Indians - are desperately poor peasants or landless labourers. Two per cent of the population owns 65 per cent of the land, while 63 per cent of the population lives below the official poverty line. Nearly half the population has no access to health care, more than half cannot read or write, and infant mortality is six times the rate in Britain. Although the country's economy is based on commodities like coffee, sugar, cotton and beef, Guatemala does have a small industrial sector. The typical factory is low technology, low wage and often owned or financed by US multinationals. Only a very small percentage of the workers in these factories are organised into trade unions.

Throughout this century political and economic power has lain in the hands of the military and big landowners. A brief period of reform between 1944 and 1954 was brought to an end when the democratically-elected President Jacobo Arbenz was ousted in a military coup engineered by the CIA and the United Fruit Company. Arbenz's 'crime' was to introduce modest proposals for the redistribution of land to poor peasants. Ever since the 1954 coup, demands for change have been ruthlessly kept in check by the security forces and government-controlled death squads. As a result, large numbers of trade unionists, peasants, priests, students and political leaders have been killed or forced into exile. Others have joined the armed opposition, the URNG (National Revolutionary Unity of Guatemala).

Hopes of reform were briefly kindled in 1985 when Presidential elections were held. Vinicio Cerezo, a Christian Democrat, became the new President. While direct repression has decreased, and trade unions and peasants have begun to organise more publicly, the power of the security forces and the landowners remains intact. Many Guatemalans feel that this is only a breathing space before the next round of repression.

1 Occupation

One Saturday in February 1984, when workers came in for the morning shift at the Coca-Cola bottling plant in Guatemala City, they found copies of the following letter from the company:

Embotelladora Guatemalteca, S.A.   18 February 1984
24 Calle 6-01, Zona 11 - Tels: 762228/30, 762669 y 762678
Cables: EGUAT, Apartado Postal 161 - Guatemala, C.A.

COCA-COLA   **7-UP**
FANTA   **GRAPETTE**

To: All employees of Embotelladora Guatemalteca, Sociedad Anónima
(Guatemalan Bottling Company Limited)

We regret to have to inform you that your contract of work is hereby terminated with effect from today, owing to the complete closure of this plant.

Unfortunately, our financial situation makes it impossible for us to continue production, and we are therefore, most reluctantly, obliged to bring your employment to an end.

It is our firm intention to make good to you any indemnity payments owing, as we have explained to your trade union representatives, and this will be done under the supervision of the Inspector of Labour.

We thank you sincerely for your cooperation during the time we have worked together in our company.

The only warning of the bankruptcy and loss of jobs had come at 9pm the previous evening. The company owner, Antonio Zash, arrived with the plant manager and a group of security guards and met the committee of STEGAC, the trade union at the plant.

'They came in,' explained Rodolfo Robles, general secretary of STEGAC, 'and without more ado informed us that as of that moment the company was closing down. We couldn't believe it, because whichever way you look at it, this is a profitable business. They told us that as far as they were concerned we could demand an audit or take it to court or do what we liked, but we wouldn't get anywhere.'

Throughout Friday night the STEGAC executive discussed what to do. Urgent messages were sent to other trade unions and to the International Union of Food and Allied Workers' Associations (IUF) in Geneva, to which STEGAC was affiliated. When the morning shift arrived, an assembly of the workers was hastily arranged. The momentous decision was taken to occupy the plant.

The climate of terror

The Coca-Cola workers knew only too well the dangers they were facing. In February 1984, Guatemala was still under direct military rule. The coup led by General Mejía Víctores in August the previous year had brought a new wave of repression in Guatemala City. Trade unionists were favourite targets for kidnapping and assassination by the security forces and death squads, while mass raids and army patrols created a climate of terror on the streets. In February alone, 47 people were assassinated and 106 kidnapped and disappeared. Three leading members of the CNT, the union federation to which STEGAC belonged, had recently been kidnapped, and one of them killed. Why were the Coca-Cola workers, and their union, STEGAC, willing to risk so much by occupying their plant?

In one sense the Coca-Cola workers had little choice. If they lost their jobs, they would stand virtually no chance of being employed elsewhere. Anyone who had worked at the Coke plant was likely to be blacklisted by CACIF, the employers' organisation.

But it was not just STEGAC's future that was at stake. The Coke workers knew themselves to be in the forefront of the fight for basic trade union rights in Guatemala. The outcome of this battle, as STEGAC leader Rodolfo Robles explained, would have a profound influence on the whole future of trade unionism in the country:

> 'The Coca-Cola workers' trade union is a vital component of the trade union movement in Guatemala. By closing down this plant, the employers were automatically destroying the union. A few months later, we reckoned, they would be using the same procedure to close down other factories where there are trade unions.'

Despite the danger there were important factors working in STEGAC's favour. For some months the Coke workers had been expecting a move against their union or its leaders and preparing to confront it. They also had one of the strongest and most militant unions in Guatemala, and enjoyed the backing of the rest of the trade union movement. Above all, they could count on a vast network of support throughout the world. To understand why this was so, we need to go back to the beginning of the Coca-Cola workers' struggle, more than a decade earlier.

2 The early years 1976 - 1980

Coca-Cola has been bottled in Guatemala since 1939. The company does not directly own or manage the plants, but has franchise contracts with local bottlers. The main plant, with a monopoly of distribution to the capital city and surrounding areas, is Embotelladora Guatemalteca S.A. or EGSA. EGSA was originally owned not by Guatemalans, but by a rich North American family, the Flemings from Houston, Texas, who had made their money in oil.

After the 1954 military coup, the existing union at EGSA was crushed. Two years later, when her husband died, Mary Fleming brought in another Texan, John C. Trotter, as company President. Trotter, a fundamentalist Christian and fervent anti-communist, commuted regularly to Guatemala in his private aircraft, and from the first was directly involved in the day-to-day running of the plant.

A new attempt to organise the Coca-Cola workers was made in 1968, but collapsed when one of the leaders, César Barillas, was kidnapped, tortured and killed. It was not until 1975 that the Coca-Cola workers again tried to form a union, at a time when trade union activity was increasing rapidly throughout Guatemala. The Coca-Cola workers themselves describe what happened the following year:

'On 24 March 1976, at 2pm, a list was posted on the company notice-board, announcing the dismissal of over 160 workers, all of them members of the union. By 4pm the same day we had decided to occupy the plant peacefully and declare a strike. The occupation lasted for 16 days.

In their desperation to destroy the union, the managers decided to call in the *pelotón modelo*, the special patrol group, who arrived in two 'Bluebird' vans and various police buses and surrounded the plant, joining forces with the plant security guards. Shouting through a megaphone, they ordered us to get off the premises immediately. Meanwhile, they were hunting for our leaders, to arrest them, but we barricaded ourselves into the garden on the street side. Then they waded into us, hitting out to right and left indiscriminately.

One group of workers was beaten really brutally, but instead of being taken to hospital, they were dragged off to secret detention centres. They didn't reappear until some time later, when we found them at the Pavón prison farm.

The strike lasted until 8 April. It was a hard time for the Coca-Cola workers. We had to sleep in the street outside the plant, in all weathers, with only beans to eat, taking turns to mount guard. We had a tremendous amount of help from the CNT federation, as well as our valiant lawyers, Marta and Enrique Torres. Thanks to their efforts, on 8 April 1976, we were woken up at 3am by fireworks and *mariachi* music. We had won, our union was registered, the 160 workers were reinstated and we all got back pay.'

6

The going gets tough

The Coca-Cola workers had won legal registration of the union and reinstatement for the sacked workers. But this was only the first round in a much longer battle. They still had to obtain recognition and bargaining rights (*convenio*) from the company. Guatemalan workers have to face a whole variety of obstacles before securing full union rights (see box). Already Trotter, the company President, was employing a number of different tactics to break the union.

Trade unions in Guatemala

In Guatemala, as elsewhere in Latin America, there are no national unions of the kind found in Britain, except among teachers and public employees. Instead, workers in industry have to organise separately within each factory and fight for both legal registration for their union (*personería jurídica*), and then for recognition and bargaining rights from their employer (*convenio*).

In 1984 there were probably no more than 75 unions in the country, representing less than two per cent of workers. Apart from the risk of death, torture, and disappearance, workers have to face more sophisticated obstacles to forming and defending a union:

● company- or government-sponsored unions or staff associations are set up whose members are paid higher wages than those in worker-initiated unions
● Executive Council members must be literate, but many very able activists are illiterate
● seasonal labourers on the plantations are not allowed to join trade unions, although they are often the worst paid and suffer appalling working conditions
● Guatemalan labour laws favour small work-place unions, so secondary picketing is outlawed. Workers in the same sector, like teachers or banana-plantation workers, cannot organise a joint action
● some trade union officials receive US-sponsored trade union courses which promote company loyalty and a commitment to company profits, and to working within the law irrespective of the nature of that law
● bureaucracy in the registration procedure often means delays of a year before a union is legally recognised
● unions can call in inspectors from the Ministry of Labour and take employers to tribunals to press for recognition, bargaining rights and protection against dismissal. In practice however, there are only a few Labour inspectors, and they and the tribunals often cave in to pressure from employers or the military. In the 1970s Labour inspectors and tribunal judges who stood firm were likely themselves to be threatened by the death squads.

Once a union is established, it may affiliate to one of a number of national federations, but these have little power and are seldom, if ever, recognised by employers. At national level, there is no single trade union centre, like the British TUC.

First, two hundred new workers were hired and offered better wages and perks on condition they did not join the union (although many did join later, when they realised how they were being used). Next, a staff association was set up under effective management control, and some of its members sent at company expense on 'labour relations' courses in Costa Rica. The association began to promote 'family festivals' and outings to the beach, all paid for by the company.

Trotter's third tactic was to establish a dozen or more companies and divide up EGSA' s activity among them. In the labour tribunals, EGSA management argued that as the workforce was employed by separate companies, one union could not represent them. Marta and Enrique Torres, the lawyers for CNT and the Coke workers, responded by filing multiple wage claims for the workers in each of the new companies, and renaming the union STEGAC (Trade Union of Workers in the Guatemala Bottling and Associated Companies). Much of 1977 was spent in protracted proceedings with the Ministry of Labour and labour tribunals, with EGSA' s management continually inventing new pretexts for delaying recognition of the union.

The last and most important of Trotter's methods of union-busting was physical violence and intimidation. In Guatemala, factory owners could hire members of the PMA, the Mobile Military Police, to act as armed guards in their plants. There was a fixed charge per guard per day, payable to the army. PMA guards were already used at EGSA, and more were now brought in. In October 1976 Manuel López Balam, one of the STEGAC leaders, was hospitalised for two weeks after one of the security guards drove a truck at him.

EGSA managers began to make explicit threats to Coke workers active in the union. On 10 February 1977 the personnel manager threatened Angel Villeda and Oscar Humberto Sarti. On 1 March, both were shot and wounded. The following day, the Coke workers' lawyers, the Torres, were seriously injured when their car was deliberately bumped and forced off the road by a jeep driven by a government employee. Much worse was to come, and it was to affect not the only Coca-Cola workers, but the whole trade union movement in Guatemala.

The rising tide

The Guatemalan trade union movment had been decimated in the wake of the 1954 coup. Membership dropped from about 27 per cent of the working population, to less than 2 per cent. But by the early 1970s there were signs of a revival as a wave of strikes by teachers, bank workers and other unions shook the country.

On 24 March 1976, the day the first occupation at EGSA began, a new broad trade union grouping was formed, called CNUS (National Committee of Trade Union Unity). Sixty five unions of industrial, service and farm workers took part, including STEGAC and most of the other affiliates of the CNT federation. CNUS gave immediate support to the Coca-Cola workers. As the strikers picketed opposite the EGSA plant, delegations arrived from other unions - sugar and corn mill workers, power workers and workers from the INCASA coffee plant (which was owned by Coca-Cola), bringing donations in cash or kind. On 5 April CNUS threatened a general strike if the 154 EGSA workers were not reinstated.

Coke workers with STEGAC song

The success of the occupation at Coca-Cola acted as a spur to other trade unionists, and throughout 1977 there were disputes in the banks, sugar mills and textile factories. Coke workers gave their support to all of these, and the brightly painted Coca-Cola delivery lorries became a familiar sight, arriving with refreshment for the pickets.

The event that really galvanised the trade union movement, and for the first time brought together peasants, industrial workers, students and the urban poor, was the march of the miners of Ixtahuacán in November 1977. Locked out by their employers when they tried to form a union, the miners decided to march the 160 miles to Guatemala City to put their case to the authorities. The march took nine days. Along the route, groups of peasants and other workers brought food and refreshment to the marchers. One of them, Luis Castillo, described their arrival in the capital:

9

'With our struggle, our weariness, our feet blistered and bleeding from the burning tarmac, we made our entrance into the capital. The people of the capital had never seen a march like this one before. Nor had we, come to that. You could see the emotion of so many people who knew we were setting an example for all. The bridges were thronged with people. Well-wishers would break through the lines to give us sodas, fruit juice and tortillas. We miners set an historic example that will never be erased from the minds of many compañeros.'

One hundred thousand people turned out to see the miners' march arrive. Marching with them were many of the Coca-Cola workers, and others from the unions affiliated to CNUS and the CNT.

On 29 May 1978 landowners and government troops massacred over 100 Indian peasants in the town of Panzós about 80 miles north-east of Guatemala City. CNUS and CUC, a recently-formed peasant federation, organised a joint protest demonstration in Guatemala City on 6 June which drew 60,000 people, including trade unionists, Indians, church groups and two bishops.

In the capital, protest and repression were escalating rapidly. A city-wide strike by bus drivers in July left tens of thousands walking to work each day. When the government tried to double the fares, riots erupted with barricades, street fighting and buses burned, leaving 31 dead and 200 wounded by the police and over 1,000 arrests.

The reign of the death squads

CACIF, the employers' organisation, and the security forces fully understood the threat CNUS represented. CNUS's founder, Mario López Larrave, was assassinated in June 1977, and a number of other CNUS activists were killed in the first months of its existence. It was against this background that John Trotter stepped up his campaign against the Coca-Cola workers. In October 1978, STEGAC general secretary Israel Márquez narrowly escaped injury when his delivery lorry was raked by machine-gun fire. He had been 'warned' by two company managers. In early December, Trotter warned that Pedro Quevedo, the STEGAC treasurer, would be killed unless he stopped his union activity. On 12 December Quevedo, one of the founders and a former general secretary of STEGAC, was shot dead while on his delivery round.

Trotter and other members of the EGSA management attended a series of meetings in November 1978 between businessmen and General Chupina, the new chief of police, to coordinate strategy against the unions. Shortly afterwards, the company hired three ex-army officers to fill the posts of chief of personnel, warehouse manager and head of security.

Lieutenant Francisco Rodas was the new chief of personnel at the Coca-Cola plant. He was described by the union as 'a former army lieutenant, dismissed from the service for drunkenness, an ex-commando instructor in the Panama Canal Zone, and an active member of the Secret Anti-

Communist Army (ESA). When interviewing workers in his office, he did so with a revolver on the desk in front of him, and a bodyguard on either side.'

ESA was one of several death squads whose activities had rapidly increased since General Lucas García became President of Guatemala in July 1978. A police spokesman told the press that ESA alone killed 3,252 'subversives' in the first ten months of 1979. The government systematically denied responsibility for such operations, laying the whole blame on 'independent anti-communist death squads'. Amnesty International reached a different conclusion: 'No evidence has been found to support government claims that "death squads" exist that are independent of the regular security services. Routine assassinations and summary executions are part of a clearly defined programme of government in Guatemala.'

A common practice of ESA was to publish death lists. One ESA communiqué placed on the list, among others, Israel Márquez, the general secretary of STEGAC, and Frank LaRue, a lawyer for the CNT.

'The Supreme Court of ESA has judged and condemned to death these cowardly, bad Guatemalans, who wish to seize control of our people and lead them into total communism. ESA has set a reasonable time limit. If, and only if, they leave Guatemala by that date and leave our people in peace, well and good. If not, sentence of death will be carried out.'

NOW OR NEVER
the SUPREME COMMAND of ESA

Throughout 1978, the Torres, STEGAC's lawyers, also received repeated death squad threats, and reluctantly left the country for exile. On 2 January 1979, the entire executive committee of STEGAC received threatening letters from ESA at their homes. The only possible source of the addresses was company files. Then, on 14 January, general secretary Israel Márquez narrowly escaped an ambush by armed men at the entrance to the EGSA plant. For the next two days troops, police and men in plain clothes descended on the plant in unmarked vehicles, looking for him. He no longer dared return to his home, and slept at a different address each night. A couple staying at his house were shot and the husband killed.

Israel Márquez could no longer go to work, live at home or safely meet with friends or union colleagues. The only course left open to him was to leave the country, and he sought asylum in the Venezuelan Embassy. Before departing for Costa Rica on 29 February 1979, the STEGAC leader wrote a moving letter to his colleagues in the union:

'I want to re-emphasise a point that you will remember has been constantly made: the union is not composed of a single person, nor even of an executive committee. Rather, THE UNION IS ALL OF US, AND EACH ONE OF US HAS RESPONSIBILITY FOR IT. The union does not exist because it is legally recognised, but rather because it represents the will of a group of workers who

11

An avalanche of killings

1979

5 April Manuel López Balam, general secretary of STEGAC, is killed by a group armed with knives and iron bars as he is delivering crates of Coca-Cola.

18 June Silverio Vásquez, an EGSA worker, is shot and wounded by a plant security guard.

5 July An attempt is made to kidnap Marlon Mendizábal, now the STEGAC general secretary.

October The 16-year-old daughter of STEGAC lawyer Yolanda Urízar is arrested, beaten, raped, tortured and temporarily blinded.

1980

15 February Armando Osorio Sánchez, an EGSA worker, is kidnapped in the EGSA plant and killed.

14 April Trotter sacks 28 workers and three union leaders. The workers stage a sit-in which is violently dispersed by the police with tear gas and machine-gun fire. When a labour inspector intervenes, he is pistol-whipped by an EGSA manager. The security guards refuse to allow the sacked workers into the plant, shooting and seriously wounding one of them.

1 May Two Coca-Cola workers are among 30 kidnapped and killed while on their way home after the traditional May Day rally. The lips of one of them, Arnulfo Gómez Segura, are slashed with a razor, and his tongue cut out and placed in his shirt pocket.

14 May The leader of the management controlled staff association, Efraín Zamora, is killed, apparently after threatening to resign.

27 May STEGAC general secretary Marlon Mendizábal is gunned to death at the bus stop opposite the plant.

20 June Lt Rodas, the personnel manager, is shot and killed by the guerrilla group FAR. STEGAC is blamed, and in reprisal STEGAC Executive member, Edgar René Aldana Pellecer, is shot and killed in the plant by Rodas' bodyguards.

21 June Two STEGAC leaders are arrested in a massive police raid on the office of the CNT federation, and disappeared.

28 June Police machine-gun entrance to EGSA plant, wounding two workers.

1 July EGSA management call police to clear out strikers. 80 members of Special Patrol Group attack and beat workers. Marcelino Sánchez Chajón and another worker are kidnapped and disappear.

believe in one solid defence which includes all our workers; this is our union organisation.'

In considering the difficult moments which we are experiencing, the fury with which the company pursues me, and all the crimes against each one of us, it is nevertheless clear that they will not succeed in destroying us; on the contrary, our union each day becomes better known to the working people of Guatemala.'

After Márquez's exile, attacks on the union multiplied. His successor as general secretary, Manuel López Balam, was killed when a group armed with knives and iron bars attacked him while he was on a delivery round. A third general secretary, Marlon Mendizábal, was machine-gunned to death the following year. In all, from April 1979 to July 1980, four workers were shot and wounded, four disappeared and seven killed (see box).

When Israel Márquez left for Costa Rica he found the Torres and other exiles already there. Together they set to work to denounce the crimes being committed in their country. As they made contact with churches, human rights groups and trade unions in other countries, they began to establish a new and powerful means of defence for the Coca-Cola workers and other trade unionists in Guatemala. Their work would act as a crucial form of support for STEGAC in what was to come.

3 Boycott Coca-Cola!

Events at the Coca-Cola plant in Guatemala had for some time been under scrutiny by a group of Coke shareholders in the US. These were several churches and religious orders who happened to own shares in the company and belonged to an organisation called the Interfaith Centre for Corporate Responsibility (ICCR). ICCR believes in using shareholders' rights to put pressure on large corporations by raising issues in public and submitting resolutions to corporation annual general meetings.

ICCR first approached the headquarters of Coca-Cola in Atlanta towards the end of 1976, to express concern about the company's bottler in Guatemala. They prepared a resolution for Coke's 1977 AGM to which the company responded by bringing Trotter to meet the shareholders, and then offering an investigation if the group would agree to withdraw their resolution. The investigation, by Coke lawyer E. Bledel, was a whitewash, and the shareholders were not convinced. In January 1978 an ICCR delegation flew to Guatemala City. Despite lavish hospitality laid on by Trotter, they had the opportunity to meet the leaders of STEGAC - who made a deep impression on them - and to sit in on the union's first *convenio*.

On receiving the news of the murder of Pedro Quevedo, the STEGAC treasurer, in December 1978, ICCR once again submitted a resolution to Coke's AGM, calling for the company to insert a code of conduct for labour relations into its contract with franchisees. By now the Torres and Israel Márquez were in Costa Rica and ICCR decided to bring them to the US for Coke's AGM in 1979. The company was taken by surprise when Márquez stood to speak. After a detailed catalogue of the murder and intimidation practised at EGSA, Márquez concluded with a simple statement which was picked up by the world's press: 'In Guatemala, Coca-Cola is a name for murder'.

Coke versus IUF

In early 1979 STEGAC had for the first time made contact with the IUF, the Geneva-based International Union of Food and Allied Workers' Associations. IUF is one of the International Trade Secretariats (ITSs), which are autonomous confederations of unions in the same industry or occupation. It had affiliates in 60 countries, but none in Guatemala. Previously, it had undertaken multi-country campaigns on behalf of the workers of several large multinationals, notably Nestlé and Unilever. In May 1979, IUF received news of the arrest of Yolanda Urízar, the new STEGAC lawyer who replaced the Torres when they were forced into exile. The federation asked its affiliates to send cables of protest to the Guatemalan government. This marked the beginning of IUF's long involvement with the Coca-Cola workers in Guatemala.

Dan Gallin, the general secretary of the IUF, was one of the members of Amnesty International's first ever fact-finding mission to Guatemala in August 1979. Amnesty had invited him because of their particular concern about the repression of trade unionists in Coca-Cola, Kern Foods and the sugar mills. The delegation's conclusion was simple: 'To be a trade unionist in Guatemala is to risk one's life.'

Dan Gallin returned from the Amnesty mission determined that the IUF must act to help the Coca-Cola workers. For the remaining months of the year various IUF committees discussed what could be done. First, on 17 December the IUF wrote to Coca-Cola to request a meeting on the situation at EGSA. Then, on 2 January, the IUF issued a circular to affiliates suggesting a boycott of tourism – a move which received backing the same month from the general conference of trade secretariats (ITSs) in London, and from the European TUC. Finally, on 18 January 1980 a meeting took place in Atlanta between senior Coke executives, Dan Gallin and several US food industry trade unionists. Israel Márquez and Enrique Torres were also present.

Ever since it received the first enquiries about EGSA, Coca-Cola headquarters in Atlanta had maintained that it assumed no responsibility for, and had no means of controlling, its independent bottlers. The IUF and the church shareholders refused to accept this stance. For them, Coke Atlanta's responsibility was clear. As Dan Gallin wrote in a letter to the corporation:

'By allowing EGSA to use your trade mark, to act as your representative in Guatemala and by deriving financial benefits from your agreement with this company, you have committed your company's image and interest. If your license holder is seen to be directly responsible for murders and other acts of violence, threats and intimidation committed against the members of the union representing the employees of EGSA, continuing cooperation between your company and this license holder constitutes complicity.'

The corporation's strategy to combat the adverse publicity seems to have been to put mild pressure on Trotter to halt the violence, hoping that either the problem would be resolved, or at least matters could wait until the franchise expired. Coke executives were particularly anxious to do nothing that might become a precedent and disturb the comfortable relationship the company had with the majority of its franchisees.

At the 1979 AGM Coca-Cola had admitted for the first time that its contract with Trotter was due to expire in October 1981, and might not be renewed. Apart from the trade union issue, Coke may have had its own commercial reasons for wanting to get rid of Trotter. Nevertheless, the company still refused to take responsibility for events at EGSA, claiming that legally it could do nothing until the franchise expired. The IUF warned that its

Coke workers during the 1984 occupation

affiliates around the world might begin to take action against the company. Coca-Cola workers in Guatemala were being killed - they could not wait until October 1981.

At the end of January 1980, the manager of Coca-Cola Sweden sought out IUF president Sigvard Nyström, a fellow Swede. Stressing that the company was doing all it could to resolve the problems in Guatemala, he asked the IUF to postpone its actions. This was the first of many meetings between local Coke managers and trade unionists in their respective countries, with the company attempting by persuasion and sometimes positive disinformation to head off boycott action and cast doubt on the wisdom of the IUF. The federation was not deceived. On 1 February 1980 it issued a circular to all affiliates, asking them to take whatever action possible to bring pressure to bear on Coca-Cola. The boycott was on.

The sparkle of death

Coca-Cola was, and is, more vulnerable to international trade union pressure than most other corporations because it has a single, simple product, marketed to virtually every consumer in three-quarters of the world (see box). Coke is highly dependent upon its image for maintaining its high sales

16

The Coca-Cola Corporation

Coca-Cola was invented in 1886 by a pharmacist from Atlanta, Georgia, called John Styth Pemberton. Pemberton was an inventor of patent medicines, among them Triplex Liver Pills and Globe of Flower Cough Medicine. The new discovery was intended as a cordial for headaches and indigestion. In 1891 Pemberton sold the business to another Atlanta pharmacist, Asa Briggs Candler, who rapidly realised the importance of his new acquisition. By 1895 Coca-Cola was being sold in every state of the US.

The company grew rapidly by licensing its product and marketing only the vital ingredient – the concentrate syrup. This was the beginning of Coke's system of franchising: the company does not normally own or manage the manufacturing operations. Instead, a local entrepreneur will put up the capital to build a bottling plant, install machinery and hire a workforce. Coca-Cola supplies only the syrup and the company 'image', and thus takes no commercial risk. Among other benefits to the company, it is able to claim that it bears no responsibility for the employment practices of Coca-Cola plants the world over, since these are 'independent bottlers' over which it has 'no control'.

'Megabrand Coca-Cola', as the present chairman R.C. Goizueta likes to call it, is undoubtedly the world's best-known trade mark. At present the company controls 44 per cent of the world's soft drink sales. It has an annual turnover of US$8.67 billion, yielding a net profit of US$934 million – virtually the equivalent of the Guatemalan government's total budget for 1987. It is the 93rd largest corporation in the world, and the seventh largest food and drink company. There are over 1,400 franchised licensees, selling Coke in 155 of the 168 countries in the world. Thirty-eight per cent of its profits is derived from operations outside the US, but Coke sees the opportunity for limitless expansion. Each North American drinks on average 806 soft drinks every year, whereas the average for the rest of the world is a dismal 118 - Coke aims to close the gap.

Coke has diversified into other products, notably Minute Maid orange juice, and television and films (it owns Columbia Pictures). In Belize, a former British colony on the Caribbean coast to the north-east of Guatemala, Coca-Cola now owns 12 per cent of the total land area, on which it plans massive citrus plantations. The environmentalist pressure group, Friends of the Earth, is campaigning against the possible damage to the Belizean rain forest if Coke proceeds.

Coke arrived in Britain in 1900, but the first bottling plant was not established until 1934. In January 1987 a new combine called Coca-Cola and Schweppes Beverages Ltd (CCS) started operations. CCS is a joint venture between Coca-Cola Great Britain Ltd and Cadbury-Schweppes and is now the largest soft drinks manufacturer in Britain. Coca-Cola Great Britain is, in turn, a wholly owned subsidiary of the Coca-Cola Corporation of the USA. CCS now make Coca-Cola, Quatro, Diet Coke, Lilt, Fresca, Hi-C and the Club Mixer, all the Schweppes drinks, Fanta, Roses Lime Juice and Kia-Ora.

continued overleaf

and market share against Pepsi-Cola and other rival companies. As explained by Mr R. Cooper, Coke's chief executive for Northern Europe, Coke management pursue a strategy of 'The Three 'A' s': Coke products should be highly Available, Affordable, and Acceptable. Any damage to this 'acceptable' image is as dangerous a threat to the company as a boycott of the product.

IUF affiliates around the world responded well to the federation's call for action. Letters began to flow to the managers of local Coca-Cola plants, and to the corporation headquarters in Atlanta. There were production stoppages at Coca-Cola plants in Finland (25-28 April), New Zealand (29 May) and Sweden (one week in late April). Stoppages were threatened in Canada, Mexico, West Germany, Mexico, Norway and Britain.

Consumer boycotts began at varying levels in many countries. Students and factory workers had Coke removed from cafeterias and vending machines. The company symbol appeared on countless stickers and posters subtly altered to show images of workers in chains or bottles of blood. Coke's favourite advertising slogan throughout Latin America was *'Coca-Cola: La chispa de la vida'* (Coke: the sparkle of life). It was the work of seconds to amend this to: *'La chispa de la muerte'* (the sparkle of death).

The CLC (Canadian TUC) set up a fund and sent money to STEGAC to support the families of those kidnapped or killed. The CLC also called on the Canadian government to halt all aid to Guatemala. In Israel, the Histradut (TUC) protested against Israeli arms sales to Guatemala; West German unions contacted major travel agencies to urge cancellation of tours to Guatemala; and in the US the United Auto-Workers urged congressmen to oppose military aid to the Lucas García government. In Britain, various unions held information meetings, sent messages of support to the Coke workers, or made representations to management at Coca-Cola plants (see box, chapter 5).

Although the measurable economic effect of these actions was very small, in almost every case they led to wide discussion of events in Guatemala and intensive 'fire-fighting' measures by Coca-Cola in an attempt to avert threatened action and to halt further unfavourable publicity. As one IUF officer put it: 'The publicity hurt the most. They live on their name. Anything that damages their image will cost them money.'

Settlement

Coke Atlanta's response to the call for a boycott was to reiterate its position that it could not intervene between union and management at a franchise plant. But at the same time Coke implied that negotiations were under way for a quick sale – which could be delayed or cancelled by boycott action. John Kirby, Coca-Cola's candidate to buy out Trotter, visited the EGSA plant in May 1980, and after surveying the climate of violence, promptly withdrew. On 23 June, the remaining STEGAC workers came out on strike, and although staff association members continued to work, production was at a virtual standstill.

On 8 July a group of senior Coca-Cola executives flew to Geneva and requested a meeting with the IUF. They offered several alternative solutions, but the IUF would accept only a buy-out which would guarantee continued employment for the EGSA workers and full recognition of the union. A new buyer was found for the plant, Antonio Zash, an executive at McCann-Erikson who had managed bottling plants for both Coke and Pepsi-Cola. Zash teamed up with Roberto Méndez, the manager of a Mexican Coca-Cola plant, and most of the finance was put up by Coca-Cola Atlanta.

On 7 September the sale of the plant to Zash and Méndez was completed, and the new owners and representatives of Coca-Cola Atlanta met the IUF in Mexico City. The new management took over the plant on 1 October, and after some delays in removing the security guards, signed a new agreement with the union on 20 December. One month later the IUF notified all affiliates that the EGSA dispute was over.

The settlement was a tremendous victory for the Coca-Cola workers and their union, STEGAC. They had forced the parent company to intervene; they rid the plant of Trotter, his managers, hired thugs and security guards; the plant remained in operation and most of the jobs were saved; the staff association was dissolved, and STEGAC itself fully recognised; and Coca-Cola was to establish a fund to provide for the families of EGSA workers who had been killed.

Perhaps most important of all, the agreement was made amidst extensive publicity, in tripartite negotiations between Coca-Cola Atlanta, STEGAC and the IUF. Even the Guatemalan government expressed satisfaction, and announced that Trotter would not be allowed to return to the country.

STEGAC appeared to have a series of solid guarantees, not least Coke Atlanta's commitment to retain overall control for five years. The church shareholders in the US could also be relied upon to resume their pressure upon the corporation if required. However, the decisive gain was that an international trade union body, the IUF, was a party to the agreement.

Finally, there were now groups of trade unionists, students and others all over the world who had heard of the Coca-Cola workers of Guatemala and who would be prepared to resume the boycott campaign against what the *Miami Herald* called 'the shapely bottle of sparkling brown liquid that has come to symbolise US world commercial hegemony'.

4 The next round 1984 - 1985

The strength of the settlement brought the Coca-Cola workers a three year truce before the next round of their battle for survival. Others were not so lucky. While in 1976-80 STEGAC formed a key part of an expanding and dynamic workers' movement engaged in a multitude of struggles, in 1984 it stood almost alone.

A movement dismembered

The mounting tide of killings during the Lucas García years had taken its toll, not only of Coca-Cola workers, but of the leaders and more active members of virtually every union in the country. In the space of two months in 1980, 44 leaders of the CNT were arrested and disappeared, never to be seen again. The first group of 27, including two from Coca-Cola, were surrounded in the CNT headquarters building on 21 June. The other 17 were seized in August at a church conference centre at Emaús, in the countryside.

No movement could for long survive the physical elimination of successive leaderships. The CNT office was closed down, and both CNT and CNUS abandoned public activity. There was still a 'Co-ordinating Committee' of CNT, but it was no longer possible to hold elections. Strikes in factories were virtually impossible after 1979.

With the urban trade union and student movements effectively paralysed, the focus of repression switched to the countryside. In February 1980, simmering discontent in the countryside boiled over into a strike by 80,000 rural workers in the sugar and cotton plantations. Although the strike was partially successful in its demand for a wage increase, some workers suspected by the military of being involved in the strike were rounded up when they returned home, and killed. These and other cases of increasing army repression were one reason why more and more workers and peasants turned to the armed opposition as the only way out of their poverty. In early 1982 the four main guerrilla groups joined together to form the URNG and were strong enough to mount a serious challenge to the state.

In March 1982 'born-again' Christian General Ríos Montt became President after a military coup, and vowed to wipe out the URNG. As a result of the army's counterinsurgency policy of attacking the civilian support for the guerrillas, 440 villages were completely destroyed, many hundreds of peasants killed, and over 100,000 forced to flee northwards into Mexico as refugees. Survivors of the onslaught were herded into new 'model village' settlements under strict army control or forcibly conscripted into 'civil patrol' militias.

20

Ríos Montt was ousted in a military coup in August 1983. His successor, General Mejía Víctores, soon renewed the assault upon trade unions and urban organisations. Four trade unionists from two sugar mills were kidnapped and went missing. At CAVISA, the factory which made bottles for Coca-Cola, Edgar Fernando García, the minutes secretary of the union, was abducted by members of the BROE (Special Operations Unit of the Police). García disappeared, and five other members of the union negotiating committee fled the country after being threatened by death squads.

The favourite targets were surviving members of the organisations that had led the popular movement in 1977-80, especially the CNT federation and CNUS. For the time being, the Coca-Cola workers were not touched. The strength of their international support had given them a degree of immunity.

Despite this new round of terror, there were signs of a tentative reemergence of the trade union movement. For example, a count of advertisements placed in the press by trade unions (a far cheaper and more common means of communication in Latin America than in Europe), showed a leap from an average of 4 per month during 1983 to 14 in January 1984, 38 in February and 36 in the first two weeks of March.

At around the same time as the Coke occupation, moves were already afoot to establish a new umbrella organisation called CONUS. At the first meeting 3 unions were present, at the next 18, and at the next 30. Although this was still far short of the 150 or so unions affiliated to CNUS at its height, STEGAC helped by providing the means of organisation and sometimes a place for meetings for other trade unions. Above all, STEGAC was a symbol of strength and survival. Its battle was a battle for the future of trade unionism in Guatemala.

Coke rethinks

The 1980 settlement was not totally satisfactory for the Coca-Cola Corporation in Atlanta. Undoubtedly the company was relieved to have got rid of Trotter, re-established production and avoided further boycotts and damaging publicity. But had this been achieved at too high a cost?

Ever since the 1980 settlement, Coca-Cola had been criticised in business circles for allowing the dangerous precedent of multinational trade union intervention (the IUF) in multinational corporation affairs. For example, an article in *Business Week* in November 1980 argued:

'A cardinal rule of labor relations for multinational corporations has always been to prevent unions from gaining enough power to negotiate on a multinational basis. The companies have refused, for example, to bargain with international labor federations. But Coca-Cola Co. apparently negotiated with the International Union of Food & Allied Workers' Associations (IUF) to resolve a dispute involving human rights and union recognition in Guatemala.

Coke denies that it "negotiated" with the IUF; Coke says that its representatives met with the IUF officials merely to keep them abreast of the

Soldiers rounding up demonstrators in Guatemala City

company's effort to find a new franchise owner. "If this isn't a negotiating situation, I don't know what is," IUF's Dan Gallin says. "Our objectives were exactly what we got."

Herbert R Northrup, director of the Wharton School's Industrial Research Unit of the University of Pennsylvania, said, "it would appear that Coca-Cola's lack of preparation and understanding of the nature of the relationships let it into a virtual de facto recognition of the IUF. They gave Gallin a big political victory." '

The same Professor Northrup drew the comparison with IUF's earlier campaigns against Unilever, which 'achieved no significant objective'. He concluded:

22

'It remains to be seen whether the Coca-Cola Company can develop a policy similar to that of Unilever. This means developing programmes to counter trouble before it becomes a national or international problem. If after such a reorganisation, Coca-Cola desires to extricate itself from its new relationship with the IUF, it may then be equipped to withstand the barrage of critical publicity the IUF would likely attempt to unleash.'

By 1984, extricating itself from its new relationship with the IUF appeared to part of what Coca-Cola had in mind.

Asset stripping

When Trotter and Mary Fleming sold EGSA to Zash and Méndez in October 1980, the real purchasers of the plant were Coca-Cola Atlanta. Virtually all the finance came from Coke. Zash and Méndez established a Panama-registered company called AICA which became the owner of the EGSA plant. The entire plant (land, buildings, machinery and transport fleet) was mortgaged to Coke Atlanta. At the same time, the two managers became owners of six beverage distribution companies which sold Coke to retail outlets outside Guatemala City.

In addition to EGSA, there were two other Coca-Cola bottling plants in Guatemala, Embotelladora del Pacífico in Retalhuleu, owned by INCASA, a Coca-Cola subsidiary, and Embotelladora Quinto in Puerto Barrios, a franchise owned by the Castillo family. Under the terms of their licenses from Coke Atlanta, these two companies were not permitted to compete with EGSA for sales in and around the capital. In neither plant was there a trade union.

Although sales were not booming, all at first appeared to be reasonably well at EGSA. During 1983, however, sales and production began to decline sharply, and the Coca-Cola workers became concerned. In November 1983, they wrote to the IUF in Geneva (STEGAC was now an IUF affiliate) to sound the first alarm about Zash and Méndez's policies. Suddenly, management was claiming that the other two Coke plants were entitled to sell beverages in EGSA territory, and at the same time deliveries outside the capital were cut, supposedly because the distributors (wholly owned by Zash and Méndez) were behind with payments. The IUF made various attempts to speak to Zash and to Coke Atlanta, but without success. The first response from the corporation was a telex on 20 February informing the IUF of the closure and bankruptcy of the plant.

Zash and Méndez had apparently been running down the company for their own financial advantage. Much of the detail of the asset-stripping was only discovered after the occupation began in February 1984, when the union leaders discovered a duplicate set of company accounts, quite different from those which had been published to justify the closure. An independent North American accountant was sent in by the IUF to conduct a separate investigation. He concluded that money had been siphoned out of EGSA by

Other unions bringing supplies to support the workers during the occupation

by various devices: the distributors (owned by Zash and Méndez) were being grossly undercharged by EGSA for supplies of the beverage. This amounted to about eight per cent of EGSA's revenue - more than the company's alleged total annual loss. In addition, various expenses of the distributors such as transport, promotion and some wages were being paid by the bottling plant. Repayments on the original debt to Coca-Cola, already a serious burden on EGSA, suddenly tripled between 1982 and 1983 suggesting that the repayments were being used to milk the plant of its financial resources. Moreover, half-a-million dollars of repayment money was unaccounted for.

STEGAC and the IUF believed that while Zash and Méndez had almost certainly been lining their own pockets, their overall strategy could not have gone unnoticed by Coke Atlanta, which must at least have known about the closure in advance and have approved it.

24

5 The Unarmed Fortress

The Coke workers took the decision to occupy the plant on 18 February 1984. A quick response from the IUF was essential if they were to survive and succeed. Within two weeks the federation had written to all affiliates calling for protests to Coke Atlanta. Jim Wilson, the IUF's journal editor, was dispatched to Guatemala City. On his return he wrote:

> 'The EGSA plant is an unarmed fortress under a state of siege in an undeclared war. Though most of the time no uniformed military or police are visible around the plant, the threat of intervention at any moment is the main concern. But the visible signs are scary enough. Occasionally a *tanqueta*, a small tank, lumbers by. Some nights noisy army trucks packed with jittery teenage soldiers roll up in front of the plant and set up quasi-roadblocks which stop passing vehicles at random. On the night of 2 March, near the main factory gate, on almost the exact spot where EGSA union general secretary Marlon Mendizábal was machine-gunned to death in May 1980, these soldiers shot and killed one passing driver, and injured his two passengers. The last night we were there we witnessed soldiers firing five volleys at a car. No-one was injured. The tyres simply exploded with a lot of noise and bullets ricocheted around the front walls and glass windows of the plant.'

Some workers' families were threatened. According to one young worker, 'the day after they announced the closure of the plant, the anonymous phone-calls began. They would ask my wife where I was, or ask to speak to her. They were trying to put the frighteners on us.'

Despite the renewed repression in the cities, this was not 1980. Although they maintained their presence in nearby streets, the security forces did not invade the EGSA plant. There was no John Trotter to urge them on: Zash and Méndez had left the country immediately after the closure and played no further part in the dispute. Both Coke Atlanta - the real owners of the plant - and the military government, had their own reasons for urging restraint.

Coke Atlanta had learned its lesson three years earlier and was anxious that there be no new martyrs to fuel international campaigns of boycott and solidarity. It probably hoped too, that in the absence of direct repression the occupation would soon wither away. In particular, the company was keen to settle the dispute before the 1984 Olympic Games, of which it was a major sponsor.

The Mejía government was faced with mounting economic difficulties and therefore badly in need of foreign aid and loans - and a better image. As part of this exercise, elections for a Constituent Assembly had been called for July 1984. Killing or disappearing Coke workers would be guaranteed to bring more bad publicity. A certain political space was therefore opening up which provided a measure of protection for the Coca-Cola workers, to which they themselves contributed by the example of their struggle.

Argument and counter-argument

On the third day of the occupation STEGAC took its case to the labour tribunals, presenting evidence that the company had broken both labour and commercial law by its sudden declaration of bankruptcy. The Ministry of Labour gave considerable support to the workers' arguments. The following week a meeting took place in Atlanta between representatives of Coca-Cola, STEGAC, Enrique Torres (the former STEGAC lawyer), the IUF and the Guatemalan Ministry of Labour. Although Coca-Cola attempted to exclude the IUF from the meeting, the company was effectively forced to talk to the international federation. Thus, within the first week, the dispute had become fully international.

In a telex to the IUF dated 21 February, Coke had claimed:

'The Company is not one of the shareholders in EGSA, although we are one of the many creditors. It is our assessment that there are various key reasons for the present financial insolvency of EGSA. These include: (1) a serious contraction of the entire soft drink market over the past three years; (2) excessive labor costs without available remedy; (3) serious undercapitalisation from its inception; (4) poor management; and (5) the overburden of the enormous debt.'

These arguments were, to say the least, hypocritical. Overwhelmingly the largest creditor was of course Coca-Cola Atlanta, and the corporation had itself arranged the initial capitalisation and the debt burden of EGSA, and was supposed to retain a continuing role in the management of the plant. The claims of a 'serious contraction' in the soft drink market were absurd, as the *Financial Times* noted at the time, while talk of 'excessive labour costs' was a thinly-veiled attempt to throw the blame on the union. STEGAC and the IUF refused to accept that the bankruptcy was genuine, arguing that the plant was commercially viable, and that it should be kept open and the jobs protected. Coke Atlanta was effectively the owner of the plant, and had agreed in 1980 to maintain a management role for five years.

The IUF was aware that this time the tactics would be different. They concluded:

'It is impossible to imagine that the company embarked on this course without taking a possible IUF reaction into account. We must therefore assume that it believes that either the IUF is not any longer in a position to meet such a challenge, or else that the company can prevail in an international confrontation. We therefore must prepare for a longer and harder struggle than we conducted in 1980.'

Keeping occupied

When the occupation began, 460 people, almost the entire Coca-Cola workforce, joined in. In the first few weeks up to 200 were inside the plant at any one time. The ten members of the STEGAC executive committee were there permanently, aware that their lives would be in danger the moment they set foot outside. They realised that they might have to be there for many months. IUF's Jim Wilson described life in the plant:

> 'Morale is very high. This is emphasised by the organised and disciplined nature of life inside. The big event of the day is one or more general assemblies when present union secretary general Rodolfo Robles or other officers give updates on events - talks with ministry officials, a new ad in the newspaper, new plans for helping those whose families are in the most precarious straits - and so on. Next, visiting unionists are introduced. After this, the day's telegrams of support are read amid much enthusiasm and cheering. Then the microphone is given to any worker who wishes to speak. Invariably this eventually turns to long reminiscences of those who fell in the 1979-80 campaign and exhortations that their deaths not now be allowed to have been in vain. The hundreds present stand attentive and silent. Then one or more members may come up to sing and to play the guitar. At the end all participate in several stanzas of the rousing STEGAC union song.
>
> The rest of the day is taken up in numerous activities. Literacy classes for the sizeable minority who never went to school. Sometimes there are entertainments like a mock beauty pageant. There are ten soccer teams. Volley ball, jogging and dominoes are participated in more informally. Even singing and guitar classes have been set up. Every day a sympathetic priest comes in from the outside to say mass before a makeshift altar surrounded by high stacks of Coca-Cola crates. We attended one such service and heard a fervent worker in prayer who raised both hands and shouted, "Glory hallelujah, praise Jehovah and may He bless the IUF."
>
> But most activities have more immediate and practical purposes. On a regular schedule, the entire plant is swept clean and trash burned. Machinery and the scores of idle trucks are inspected. There are often statements to be written, leaflets to be run off, and attempts (usually unsuccessful) to break through to the local media.'

Gradually, however, financial pressures began to appear, and the true nature of the 'siege' became clearer. On 8 March an advertisement appeared in the Guatemalan press inviting EGSA employees to go to the Metropolitan Bank, with proof of identity, to receive their redundancy pay. STEGAC replied in an advertisement the following day:

> 'We emphatically deny that EGSA is closed. What is taking place is an illegal lock-out by the owners. While the company is under summons to appear before the Labour Tribunals, no worker can be legally dismissed. The redundancy pay offered in an advertisement appearing in one morning paper is merely another attempt to destroy the unity of the workforce.'

A few of the workers, mainly office staff, accepted redundancy pay. The amounts on offer (from US$2,000 to US$4,000) were very large by

27

Guatemalan standards, certainly more than enough to tempt the faint-hearted. Some families were facing mounting debts and risked eviction from their homes for rent arrears. The special pensions for the widows and orphans of the previous dispute, established as part of the 1980 settlement, had stopped with the closure. Some workers had loans that had been underwritten by the company, and these were now called in. STEGAC set up a welfare commission to help those families in greatest need. The plant cafeteria (built after 1980 and dedicated to the memory of Pedro Quevedo, the union's first general secretary) provided at least one good meal a day and this was extremely important in maintaining morale.

Meanwhile, the telephone, electricity and water were in danger of being cut off because of unpaid bills. By 20 May, 58 workers had accepted redundancy pay and the union's funds were exhausted. Nevertheless, morale remained good, sustained by the fine example of the STEGAC executive, whose members remained in the plant 24 hours a day, and by the discipline of the commissions and activities organised by the union.

Outside help

The occupation at EGSA was both a reflection of the new mood of determination in the trade union movement and a major stimulus to it. This in part explains why so much help in cash and kind flowed into the EGSA plant every day. As IUF's Jim Wilson described:

> 'While we were there, we saw provisions come in from other food plants, a sugar mill, chemical and textile factories, a laundry workers' union, bank employees and a number of other organisations. One delegation of a banana workers' union arrived after a 300-kilometer journey over rough dirt roads through mountains and jungle. Another day, a truck appeared with dozens of eggs - a gift of the semi-clandestine Democratic Socialist Party of Guatemala.'

Now help began to flow also from abroad, as IUF affiliates all over the world started to send in cash. From 25 to 28 March a delegation of US food industry trade unionists visited Guatemela, bringing with them US$8,000 to add to the US$4,000 already sent by the IUF. The money was used to buy food and to support families in need. In early May a delegation from Canada brought further aid.

The IUF followed its first circular on 5 March by establishing a solidarity fund, and asking affiliates to make representations to local Coca-Cola plant managements in their own countries as well as to Atlanta. It also asked affiliates to 'prepare for a boycott of Coca-Cola products, wherever appropriate in cooperation with community groups, solidarity and action groups, etc, and to prepare for selective action against production and distribution of Coca-Cola products'. By 3 April, messages of support for STEGAC had arrived from Belgium, Bermuda, Brazil, Cyprus, Japan, Mexico, Norway, Panama, Switzerland, Uruguay, USA and Venezuela and the UK (see box).

UK Solidarity

Trade unions in Britain took part in the first IUF boycott campaign in support of the Coke workers in 1980. The TGWU, General and Municipal Workers (GMWU) and ASTMS all made representations to management at Coca-Cola plants in Britain. The TGWU and the Tobacco Workers Union sent protests to the Guatemalan government. USDAW workers held a meeting about Guatemala at the Belfast Coke bottling plant in May. G&MWU held information meetings at distribution and bottling plants. TGWU threatened a full production stoppage. A stong resolution in support of the Guatemalan workers was also passed at the 1980 TUC Conference.

In 1984 these actions went further. Within a month of the occupation starting, TGWU had sent cables of support to STEGAC and of protest to Coca-Cola and the Guatemalan authorities. Shop stewards at Coke bottling plants in northern England, Scotland and Wales sent similar messages. Other messages of protest were sent by ASTMS, the Bakers, Food and Allied Workers, USDAW, Tobacco Workers and the United Road Transport Workers' Union. The TGWU held several meetings with European representatives of the Coca-Cola Corporation and hounded them with frequent letters and telexes right up to the time of the settlement in February 1985.

IUF affiliates in Britain sent contributions to the IUF's solidarity fund, based on a levy of just over 3p per member; the video 'The Real Thing' was shown to Coke workers and to the general public; and the Greater London Council (GLC) stopped buying Coca-Cola for its restaurants, bars and cafeterias; and the development agency, War on Want, sent £2,000 to the families of the Coca Cola workers. Letters of support were also sent from solidarity and human rights groups. A British human rights worker who visited the Coke plant in October 1984 was shown the country files of letters received by STEGAC. 'In our darkest hours,' explained one official, 'we just take out these letters and read them to each other to keep up our morale.'

In May, the IUF reported another US$21,000 in donations received, the main contributions coming from Norway and West Germany, but this had already been distributed to STEGAC families for food. More was needed. Members of theatre and film technicians unions in the US gave their services free to make a film about the occupation (*The Real Thing*) which was later shown to hundreds of solidarity meetings in many countries. Production stoppages of Coca-Cola were now being planned in Australia, Norway and Sweden.

Coke responds

Coke Atlanta reacted to the increasing pressure by sending groups of senior managers to talk to the main organisations involved - with the exception of the IUF. Company spokesmen explained that for reasons of 'principle' they did not want to speak to the IUF. First, they went to see the religious shareholders of the ICCR, who had remained in touch with STEGAC ever since 1978, and who had once again intervened at the corporation AGM. Shortly afterwards Coke delegations visited the Norwegian, Swedish, German, Belgian and Dutch affiliates of the IUF. On 7 May, at the congress of the Danish Food Workers Union in Copenhagen, the Coca-Cola executives found themselves confronting Dan Gallin and other IUF leaders, invited by the Danes.

By now, the company had changed its position. It was no longer arguing that Coca-Cola production was non-viable in Guatemala City. Instead the spokesmen claimed that the plant would be re-opened as soon as a suitable buyer could be found, and that the existing workforce would be rehired and the union recognised. In the meantime, the US$1.8 million fund deposited in a Guatemalan bank was not for redundancy payments but for interim wage payments to EGSA workers until the plant re-opened; it was due to the urging of the company that the Guatemalan government had used 'utmost restraint'.

The IUF was suspicious:

> 'At just about the same stage of the campaign in 1980 the company was contacting our affiliates saying that a solution was imminent. In reality such assertions served the sole purpose of demobilising and slowing down solidarity action. There was no genuine response from the company until it realised that it could not prevent solidarity action except by settling.
>
> The IUF Executive committee has asked all affiliated unions for solidarity action "with all means at their disposal and to the full extent of all legal possibilities". This means production stoppages, stopping transport, distribution and sale of Coca-Cola products, boycotts, consumer information campaigns, negative publicity or any combination of these. Do not delay any solidarity action you may have been considering. The right time is now.'

6 Endgame

Boycott action began immediately, and spread rapidly. On 7 May production stopped at 13 different Coke bottling and canning plants in Norway. In Italy, several short stoppages occurred at Coca-Cola plants while workers met to hear reports on the situation in Guatemala. Austrian unions wrote to the local Coca-Cola management threatening action. In Mexico, ten different bottling plants held solidarity strikes for three days each on a rotating basis, while in Sweden all five IUF affiliates staged a full production and sales stoppage for three days.

News of further union action plans reached Atlanta: a week-long production, sales and distribution stoppage in Norway due to commence on 4 June; an indefinite stoppage to begin in Denmark on 15 June; and, probably most worrying of all, a national boycott campaign by a coalition of IUF affiliates and church and consumer groups scheduled to start in 16 US cities on 21 May. The Presidents of around 19 North American unions publicly announced that they would support the boycott.

The company was ready for a tactical retreat. Under pressure from the US unions, it agreed to a meeting in Costa Rica with representatives of STEGAC, the IUF and the Guatemalan Ministry of Labour. After two days of intense negotiation a settlement was signed on 27 May. Coca-Cola agreed to sell EGSA to a 'reputable' buyer and to prevent the two non-union Coca-Cola plants in Guatemala from poaching EGSA's sales territory; it guaranteed that the new owners would recognise STEGAC and the existing bargaining agreement; it also guaranteed to employ and pay the surviving 350 workers (96 had by now taken redundancy pay) until the plant re-opened; finally, the plant would re-open with all 350 employees and no-one would be laid off unless sales failed to reach an agreed target within 60 days.

While the agreement represented a considerable victory for STEGAC, it contained one concession to the company: the IUF was not a party to the agreement and therefore would no longer retain quite the same watchdog role it had had since 1980. But there was another, less obvious catch: no buyer had yet been found and Coke Atlanta refused to take over the plant in the meantime. Would the new owner accept and abide by the terms, and if not, would the US company assume responsibility? The IUF felt that it had got the best deal available even if its own formal role was no longer recognised: 'The only real guarantee lies in the capacity of our affiliated unions and of our friends for quick mobilisation.' In the light of the agreement, the boycott was called off.

Under the terms of the agreement, US\$252,000 was allocated for back-pay for the workers (about US\$240 per month each). They could also claim the

Official re-opening of the Coke bottling plant, 1 March 1985

remainder of the redundancy fund set up by Zash and Méndez at the time of the closure which should suffice in lieu of wages until the plant re-opened. According to company calculations, there was enough to last until September.

In the event, no new buyer appeared. When the IUF's regional secretaries visited the plant in mid-August, they reported that although the morale of the workers had understandably fallen, a sense of calm prevailed. One major problem was medical expenses as there is no national free health service in Guatemala. Since national insurance payments were no longer being made by the company, the workers and their families had to pay for all medical care. The workers were still determined to see the occupation through to the end.

Settlement

As September wore on and still no buyer appeared, the IUF warned its affiliates to gear up once more for boycott action, and gave the company an ultimatum to come up with a solution by 10 October. Coke Atlanta now claimed to be negotiating with three potential buyers, and the federation reluctantly decided to allow more time, while keeping its affiliates on standby for a resumption of the boycott. By early November, with negotiations with buyers still in progress, STEGAC's funds were completely exhausted, and the

IUF once more appealed for contributions.

Finally, on 9 November Coca-Cola announced that it had signed a letter of intent to sell the plant to a consortium led by Carlos Porras González, a reputable economist who had run businesses in El Salvador. The first meetings between the union and the new prospective owner were not encouraging. Porras claimed to have no knowledge of the Costa Rica agreement of 27 May. He said that he had no obligation to former employees; that the union no longer existed since its members had collected their redundancy pay; and that he would hire fewer workers and at a lower wage. The IUF was outraged and demanded a new meeting with Coke Atlanta.

The company refused: the 27 May agreement had only been an 'understanding'; the matter was now entirely for negotiation between the workers and the new owner; and the company was not willing to intervene, nor to hold further meetings with the IUF.

Porras was playing a double game: holding off against Coca-Cola to negotiate the cheapest terms and the least possible commitment to what he saw as hangovers from the previous regime at EGSA; and pushing the union to accept more redundancies. Meanwhile the market for Coca-Cola in much of the capital city was being supplied by the non-union plants in Retalhuleu and Puerto Barrios.

For STEGAC and the Coca-Cola workers the situation was very serious. Christmas came and went, with still no settlement. Most had received no pay since September, and the funds sent by the IUF were only enough to cover basic necessities. Only their discipline, their confidence in the IUF and the steady stream of messages of support from abroad sustained them.

Finally, on 1 February, just over two weeks short of the anniversary of the start of the occupation, an agreement was signed. Porras' consortium would operate the plant under a new name, Embotelladora Central SA. EGSA had been declared bankrupt and the company dissolved. STEGAC, too, was formally dissolved, but a new union, STECSA, was formed from the membership of the old and recognition was guaranteed. Initially only 265 workers were re-employed, but if production and sales reached agreed levels, more would be hired with preference given to former employees.

The settlement was a good one, although it was less than the union had hoped for after the meeting in Costa Rica. All sides had made some concessions: the union had allowed some redundancies; Porras had given full recognition to the union and higher manning levels than he wanted; and Coca-Cola had assumed some of the financial responsibilities of the bankrupt EGSA.

Repair work began in February and work officially resumed on 1 March. On 20 March, the first bottles came off the production line and two days later the plant was officially re-opened in the presence of the Guatemalan President, Mejía Víctores and the US Labour Attaché. STECSA was recognised by the company and received legal registration on 11 April. Early production figures were good and 52 more workers were taken on. STECSA signed an agreement releasing Coca-Cola from its obligations under the agreement reached in Costa Rica the previous May, and received a further US$250,000 to cover back pay and compensation for those made redundant.

In an advertisement inserted in Guatemalan newspapers STECSA gave its verdict on the victory:

> 'We want to make clear to posterity that the decisive factor in winning this solution to our problems was the unity shown in the moral and material solidarity given to our union both from within our country and internationally by our brothers and sisters in many countries. A vital role was played by the IUF.
>
> Sisters and brothers, workers of different countries the world over, members of churches, fellow Guatemalan workers: this victory is yours, because your belief in the struggle for workers' just demands has been vindicated.'

The power of example

The occupation at EGSA had begun in the midst of renewed repression of trade unionists, which continued throughout the period of the dispute. In March 1984 the former general secretary of the Diana confectionery factory escaped kidnapping but with serious gunshot wounds, and sought asylum in the Belgian Embassy. Four more trade unionists were kidnapped in mid-May. In January 1985 Carlos Carballo Cabrera, a leader of the trade union federation CUSG (ICFTU affiliated) was kidnapped and tortured. A leader of the Ray-O-Vac battery workers union and two from the El Salto sugar mill were kidnapped and disappeared. Another worker from the CAVISA glass factory was kidnapped on 17 February 1985 and found dead on 13 March. He had been tortured. Why were the Coca-Cola workers not touched?

Undoubtedly their greatest defence was their international support from the IUF, from the ICCR shareholders and from Coke consumers all over the world. Coke Atlanta was probably telling the truth when it claimed to have urged the utmost restraint on the Guatemalan government: its own vital image and reputation were at stake, and the IUF had given ample evidence in April 1984 of its ability to generate a powerful and damaging campaign of publicity and boycott.

Although the Guatemalan military undoubtedly wanted to destroy the union, they recognised that this time the tactics had to be different. With elections promised and a pressing need for foreign aid, they could not afford to go back to being the pariahs of the international community. Like Coke Atlanta, they believed the union's resolve would crumble as time passed.

Both the government and the corporation were wrong. The Coke workers' struggle proved to be exceptional in the labour history of Guatemala – and perhaps anywhere in the world – for the remarkable persistence with which a group of workers pursued the right to form a trade union for more than nine years. The key factor behind the success of the year-long occupation in 1984 was the extraordinary discipline of STEGAC's members and its leadership. The morale of the occupation was sustained by the permanent presence of the

STEGAC executive committee and the daily routine of maintenance, cleaning, guard duty, assemblies, and education and leisure activity. As a result, only a few workers accepted redundancy pay.

Finally, STEGAC was sustained throughout the occupation by the involvement and support of other Guatemalan unions. They recognised that if STEGAC was destroyed, their own tentative efforts to revive union activity would be greatly jeopardised. During the occupation, the EGSA plant became a safe meeting place and a nerve centre for other trade unions. As a member of the British Parliamentary delegation witnessed in October 1984:

'At very short notice STEGAC organised a meeting for us at the plant of some 30 trade unionists representing ten different unions. The leaders wanted us to know what the general conditions of the Guatemalan workers were like. Two things impressed us about the meeting: first, the way the leaders did not take the floor, but let the rank-and-file speak for themselves; and second, the way the various members each explained how they had suffered from the repression. A wide cross-section of trade unions including the municipal workers, university students and workers in sugar mills, textiles and glass, had all lost leaders. Their crime? All of them were involved in some kind of negotiation with management or were simply demanding the right to form a workers' trade union.'

Real to Reel Film Productions Inc.

Epilogue, 1987

Relative peace has prevailed at the Coca-Cola plant since March 1985. The IUF reported in May 1987 that the agreement was still holding. An American journalist who visited the plant found the spirit of activity and organisation very much alive. Chorus groups, union education classes and english courses were all in progress, while the union front office was 'usually crowded with Coke workers, their friends and children, and organisers from other unions arriving to exchange ideas'.

The attempts to form the new trade union grouping called CONUS did not bear fruit, but in February 1985 a new independent union grouping, UNSITRAGUA, was founded with the strong support of the Coca-Cola workers. UNSITRAGUA has become firmly established with some 30 member unions, representing about 35,000 workers. In 1986 it succeeded in calling the first May Day rally in Guatemala since 1980, and in early 1987 it joined other unions in publicly demanding an increase in the minimum wage, an agrarian reform and an investigation into human rights violations.

Five more Guatemalan unions have affiliated to the IUF: the union at the Chiclés Adams chewing gum factory, the Cervecería Nacional brewery workers' union, and the unions at the Finca Mirandilla sugar mill, the Licoría Quezalteca, and the Tabacalera Centroamericana. The IUF has established an office in Guatemala City and appointed Rodolfo Robles, the former general secretary of STEGAC, as their representative.

During the time of the occupation, other social sectors were beginning to organise. In mid-1984 the relatives of the disappeared prisoners of Guatemala formed the Mutual Support Group (the GAM). One of their leaders, Nineth de García, is the wife of Fernando García, the minutes secretary at the CAVISA glass factory kidnapped in February 1984. Nineth is one of many women in the GAM whose relatives had been active trade unionists. The GAM has initiated a series of protests, hunger-strikes and demonstrations which, despite the brutal murder of two of their leaders, continue to this day and have won widespread support from church and human rights groups throughout the world. In 1986 the GAM were nominated for the Nobel Peace Prize by 56 British MPs including Neil Kinnock.

In January 1986 an elected government under Christian Democrat President Vinicio Cerezo replaced the military dictatorship of Mejía Víctores. The new government has introduced few, if any, measures that would help the poor majority. More than half of the work force do not have a permanent job, and this seriously hinders union organisation. Many workers are desperate for work and fear any contact with a union would cost them a job.

Although the violence is less than before, killings and disappearances continue, and the military structures responsible for them remain fully operational. No military officer has been brought to trial for human rights offences nor dismissed from his post. A number of trade unionists have been killed under the new regime, and as a British Parliamentary delegation reported in 1987, 'rank-and-file and potential activists simply do not believe it is safe to engage in open trade union activity'. Many Guatemalans believe that the security forces are simply biding their time until the trade union movement recovers its strength. As Dan Gallin, general secretary of the IUF, warns:

'No battle is ever permanently won, just as there are no permanent defeats. In Guatemala, and elsewhere in the world, we can take nothing for granted. There will be other, more difficult battles. Let us therefore always keep in mind what it takes to win.

It takes unity, courage and staying power on the front line: if the Guatemalan workers had not stood fast, international support would have been to no avail. It takes coalition-building: church groups, human rights organisations, public interest and solidarity groups as well as other unions were our most valuable allies. It takes money, lots of it, and the ability to raise it quickly. It takes organisation: without a permanent, established, tried and proven network of solidarity and action, local struggles will be crushed and wasted. Finally, it takes internationalism: the clear understanding that the battle of one union, however small and remote from one's own country, makes a difference to all workers wherever they are.'

Abbreviations

AFL-CIO American Federation of Labor - Congress of Industrial Organisations

BROE Special Operations Unit (of the Police) / *Brigada de Operaciones Especiales*

CACIF Chamber of Agriculture, Commerce, Industry and Finance / *Comité Coordinador de Asociaciones Agrícolas, Comerciales, Industriales y Financieras*

CNT National Workers Confederation / *Central Nacional de Trabajadores*

CNUS National Committee of Trade Union Unity / *Comité Nacional de Unidad Sindical*

CONUS Coordinating Committee of National Organisations of Trade Union Unity / *Coordinadora Nacional de Unidad Sindical*

CUC Committee for Peasant Unity / *Comité de Unidad Campesina*

CUSG Confederation of Guatemalan Trade Union Unity / *Confederación de Unidad Sindical de Guatemala*

EGSA Guatemala Bottlers Ltd. / *Embotelladora Guatemalteca Sociedad Anónima*

ESA Secret Anticommunist Army / *Ejército Secreto Anticomunista*

FAR Rebel Armed Forces / *Fuerzas Armadas Rebeldes*

ICCR Interfaith Centre for Corporate Responsibility

ITS International Trade Secretariat

IUF International Union of Food and Allied Workers' Associations

PMA Mobile Military Police / *Policía Militar Ambulante*

STEGAC Trade Union of Workers in the Guatemala Bottling and Associated Companies / *Sindicato de Trabajadores de Embotelladora Guatemalteca, Anexos y Conexos*

STECSA Trade Union of Workers in the Central Bottling Company Coca-Cola / *Sindicato de Trabajadores de Embotelladora Central S.A. Coca-Cola*

URNG National Revolutionary Unity of Guatemala / *Unidad Revolucionaria Nacional Guatemalteca*

Guatemala Committee for Human Rights

The Guatemala Committee for Human Rights (GCHR) campaigns on behalf of the thousands of disappeared Guatemalans, including many trade unionists, whose relatives have come together in the Mutual Support Group for the Relatives of the Disappeared (GAM).

GCHR has jointly produced a photo-exhibition portraying trade union conditions in Guatemala and the rest of Central America. This exhibition, together with other exhibitions, videos and tape-slides, is available for hire. GCHR also produces the quarterly *Central America Report,* and distributes a wide range of leaflets, books, posters and cards.

GCHR staff keep in close contact with partners in the Guatemalan trade union movement and human rights organisations. We arrange tours of visiting speakers, including trade unionists, and staff members are also available to speak at branch meetings.

For details of how you can help GCHR to stop the murder and disappearance of more trade unionists in Guatemala, write to:

Guatemala Committee for Human Rights, 83 Margaret Street, London W1N 7HB. Tel: 01 631 4200.

Guatemala Working Group

The Guatemala Working Group (GWG) supports the popular organisations and groups which demand a just and constructive future for the majority of Guatemalans, and works to increase awareness in the UK of their problems and needs.

In 1982 four armed resistance groups united to form the National Revolutionary Unity of Guatemala (URNG). The URNG demands:

★ an end to repression, and guarantees of life and peace
★ an end to the economic and political domination of the rich Guatemalan elite and overseas investors
★ an end to cultural oppression and discrimination, and equality between Indian and non-Indian, women and men
★ full representation in a new, popular democratic society
★ an international policy of non-alignment, on the basis of the self-determination of all peoples.

The GWG supports the URNG's demands and the struggle of the Guatemalan people for national liberation. Your membership fee entitles you to the quarterly *Guatemala Update* and other occasional materials. Individuals: £6 (OAP and claimants £3). Affiliation: £20 (national), £10 (branch).

GWG, c/o 1, Amwell Street, London EC1R 1UL.

War on Want

War on Want is a British development agency, which supports projects and campaigns against poverty in Africa, Asia and Latin America.

War on Want has provided assistance to the development projects of the Guatemalan poor since the earthquate in 1976. At present we are helping the trade union federation, UNSITRAGUA, in its poverty-related projects. The repression of the last decade has deprived the trade union movement of many of its experienced leaders. War on Want is supporting a programme which gives trade unionists on opportunity to study Guatemalan history and basic economics while improving their literary and technical skills. Our work also includes health and production projects with people displaced by the war, many of them widows, and with peasant associations who are trying to reconstruct their communities.

For further information about War on Want and its projects, contact:

War on Want, 37-39, Great Guildford Street, London SE1 0ES.

New LAB books

Guatemala: False Hope, False Freedom

Draws upon recent research in Guatemala by the author, James Painter, to examine the enduring chasm between the rich and the poor, the continuing counterinsurgency campaign, and the policies of President Cerezo's Christian Democrat party.

Published jointly with the Catholic Institute for International Relations.

Price (inc. post and packing) £5.50

The Great Tin Crash: Bolivia and the World Tin Market

Tells the story of tin: from the rise of the tin can to the collapse of the world tin market in October 1985, and its impact on the mineworkers and their families in Bolivia.

'We recommend it to be read by all mineworkers unions.' Miners International Federation.
Price (inc. post and packing) £3.70

Other books on Central America

Promised Land: Peasant Rebellion in Chalatenango, El Salvador. £8.25 (inc. p&p)
Honduras: State for Sale. £4.25 (inc. p&p)
Under the Eagle: US Intervention in Central America and the Caribbean. £6.95 (inc. p&p)

For a complete list of LAB books write to LAB, 1 Amwell Street, London EC1R 1UL.

Latin America Bureau

The Latin America Bureau is a small, independent, non-profit making research organisation established in 1977. LAB is concerned with human rights and related social, political and economic issues in Central and South America and the Caribbean. We carry out research and publish books, publicise and lobby on these issues and establish support links with Latin American groups. We also brief the media, organise seminars and have a growing programme of schools publications.

Printed in the USA
CPSIA information can be obtained
at www.ICGtesting.com
JSHW071952120624
64681JS00030B/616